Tea with the Taliban

Tea with the Taliban
Owen Gallagher

Published 2012 by
Smokestack Books
PO Box 408, Middlesbrough TS5 6WA
e-mail: info@smokestack-books.co.uk
www.smokestack-books.co.uk

Tea with the Taliban
Owen Gallagher
Copyright 2012, by Owen Gallagher, all rights reserved
Cover image: James Cianciaruso
Author photograph: Judy Shapter

Printed by
EPW Print & Design Ltd

Middlesbrough
moving forward

ISBN 978-0-9568144-7-0

Smokestack Books is
represented by Inpress Ltd
www.inpressbooks.co.uk

Acknowledgements are due to the editors of the following publications where some of these poems were first published: *Ambit, Edinburgh Review, Iota, Poetry Ireland Review, PN Review, Poetry Scotland, Red Poets, The Gutter, The North, The SHOp, The Stinging Fly* and Alan Morrison (ed), *The Robin Hood Book: Poets in Support of the Robin Hood Tax.*

Thanks go to Graham Fawcett at the London Poetry School, and the 'pollinators' – the Pitshanger Poets.

Flowers for Ruth

Contents

Hope guard us from despair,
lead us out of passivity,
stocks, shares.

The Work Ethic

Democracy is vulnerable to viruses,
health problems, cancers; to having
its legs blown away, its tongue severed.

It can be seen on crutches at demonstrations,
on Zimmer frames in workplaces.
It never applies for a sick-note

or a chance to doss on a beach. When depressed
it thinks of its childhood in Greek states,
teenage years in communes.

You'd think it would seek a pension
but it wakes daily to a bowl of porridge,
goes off to work whistling.

Emma Goldman

Labouring through box after box of ballot-papers
I came upon a note attached to one in a hand

I recognised as Emma's, pleading,
spoil them; make a camp-fire out of them,

use them as padding for your saddle,
then ride out to join me!

Without hesitating I struck a match for Anarchy
and lit out on horseback

past a world I knew, galloped towards Emma,
her arms opened like a wishbone.

On Trotsky's Anniversary

I raised the ice-axe and thought of Mercader
bringing it down on Trotsky's skull

and red spilling all the way to Russia,
seeping upwards onto Stalin's hands.

Friends and lovers play double-agents,
Mercader with Trotsky.

My unfaithful wife's hand greets
another's under our table.

Mine tightens on the kitchen ice-axe.
I bring it down fast, hard, on

a slab of ice. Blood spurts from my finger
like a fountain into her lover's glass.

Tea with the Taliban

We holed up in a village house in Helmand,
our radio silent.
Young men beckoned us to sit.

Children played upstairs.
We took our fingers off the triggers.
The tea tasted of Wrigley's Gum.

We offered cigarettes, left refreshed.
That night we were ordered
to raid the house.

It was empty. A kettle boiled.
The smell of mint forced us
to sit and drink.

Crack Head

I never hesitated, as we exchanged fire,
to be the first to leap into the air
and race, foolhardily, across the Afghan sky

expecting others to follow.
I never thought I would fall out of the sky
on the heads of soldiers in my squad,

be a target for the Taliban. I thought
only of the sniper, who pinned us down,
watching the soles of my boots zigzagging

above and me staring down, his mouth filled
with so many bullets I was forced to reload.

The Mind Hospital

My father uses his tongue for swallowing;
he has given up on speech and behaves

as if he is back in Helmand under interrogation
by the Taliban. At the stroke of four,

when I leave the ward, a soldier in pyjamas
checks his imaginary rifle and presents arms.

Unaware of his rank, I respond, 'All correct,
soldier,' in a drill sergeant's way. He escorts me

to the main exit and inquires if I wish
to be accompanied. 'No thank you, soldier,'

I reply. He salutes and marches back
to his post, awaits another mission.

My father's mind is full of land-mines,
his finger jerks an imaginary trigger.

The Afghan Rope Trick

Everyone in the regiment were shocked
by O'Niell's rope-trick on guard duty.
Where would he have descended to in this Afghan desert?
If ever a soldier was admired for turning
corn into alcohol, it was O'Niell. There were
no tracks, no note saying Sorry; only

his laced up boots, his rifle protruding from the sand
and tags hanging from the trigger,
were left where he had been posted.
He would peer past snipers, wade
in the River Tullaghabegely and catch
Donegal salmon in his hands.

In the Garden of Eden, Iraq

When I peer into the eyes
of Sergeant Farouk
I feel him curled up against me

at night, no longer the soldier
with notches on his rifle
who forces our regiment

to train barefoot in the red-hot sand,
but the one who brings grapes
at sunset, water and oil,

undoes the laces on my boots.

Fitness Test

I rise, though I have not worked for months,
shave and dress. I am unable to impress employers
with the army medals on my chest.

I do not resort to prayers. The weather girl each morning
keeps me from despair. A new front might force
up employment figures, shares.

Having donned my Primark suit and pocketed
the CV, I set out on foot, drop my life off
in front of anyone who will take a look.

No bodyguard or security posts to fill, I consider
my only skill and ring World Security Zone
who ask if I am fit enough to kill.

Waging Peace

After a lifetime waging peace,
we waved our placards
to greet the platoons of youth
that marched to join us.

Words and looks from bystanders
bounced off us
as if hitting a flak-jacket.

I felt guns would melt
into combine harvesters,
children's slides,
buckets to draw water from wells.

The Unofficial Exhibit

The one-armed soldier's hand extends, not
for him to be hauled back from where he has,
in the past, fallen, or to be shaken, but
to beg for loose change. His beret lies
empty. A platoon of six-year olds spy
his medals, leave sandwiches and crisps,
salute and march into The Museum of War.

The streets of London are paved with ex-soldiers,
from the Falklands to Afghanistan,
in hand to hand combat with themselves.
They are concussed by war. No truce
or curfew is declared. There is no bandage
to cover memory. Each night they are positioned
at the bins of restaurants, cat-nap with
their nightmares in doorways.

At dawn they tour the city with upturned
palms. The soldier's memory is the enemy.
It is lined with booby traps. He has no words
to fire. An official of the Museum presents
visitors on leaving with a questionnaire:
'Improving Service and Exhibits.'

Yalta

Poised over a map of Europe, three figures rearranged
borders with pins. Under coffee mugs and ashes
from Churchill's cigars countries disappeared.
There was a boom in coffins and land for graveyards.

Outside, the dead kept survivors awake.
Millions were displaced inside their minds.
Amputees sat on corners and begged, *What
next?* Prayers rose and fell. Gods were on vacation.

An iron curtain was drawn that only birds and missiles
could cross. Stalin's claim to Poland hardened
as did Roosevelt's arteries.

Feeding the Polar Bears

Let us requisition a container ship
and then invite, in a national poll,
the nomination of public figures
to walk its gangway.
There is no shortage of candidates.

We will have no appeal procedure,
first-class cabins or crew.
The ship will be remote-controlled,
its destination not disclosed.

There will be no provisions, lifeboats
or landing-rights.
There will be icebergs.
Starving polar bears
will swim towards survivors.

Serving my Redundancy Notice

I sweep up crumpled papers, wipe
sweat and dust from benches, apply vinegar to stubborn stains
after another taxing night in the Commons.

Tick, tick, goes the clock. Hunched
in the Prime Minister's place I rehearse how I'll inform
my wife of my redundancy.

My knuckles turn white at the Dispatch Box.
I rage against a world that deprives people of work,
handcuffs them to hunger. I think

to plant a timed device as I unblock loos,
wipe graffiti from stalls, cycle to lie beside
my restless wife. Tick, tick, tick goes the bomb.

The Good Samaritan

Boarding a bus in Nazareth, I aid an old woman
who has an infant bandaged to her back

and wedge her black bin-bag beneath her seat.
I peer out to where Gabriel visited Mary

and Jesus whittled himself into the son of God.
We drove past Cana where I prayed my water

would be transformed into wine. The bus hiccupped
to a halt. The driver screamed. In Hebrew? Arabic?

Passengers fled. I stood. *Bomb! Bomb!* He yelled
in English. I bolted, as if the walls of the Red Sea

had risen and were about to fall on us. Security forces
interrogated me in their jeep about the Solidarity

with Palestine leaflet in my jacket, the black
bin-bag, ticking on the bus, and my Irish name.

Listening to Angels at a Workshop on Earth

God does not believe in holding back floods,
or catching bullets as they leave their chambers.
Darwinian by nature, he supports
the survival of the slickest, depends on a surplus

of the poor. There is a backlog of prayers he is unable
to clear. He works closely with the police and has dismissed
petitions to create a parliament of angels.
He wears a bulletproof vest. No one suggests

retirement or a severance package. Heaven is full
of phonetaps. God's sons argue for a Republic.
He was last seen in the sky trailing a drip-feed on a trolley.

The Holy Family

My father carried two giants in his wallet:
Marx and Lenin, family kept close
to interpret the world. 'We are not in awe of

your father's Gods', mother would say,
as she swept money-lenders and priests from the door.
Her purse contained a gallery of our faces.

Though father and mother had different views,
both, according to their ability, could love.

On Behalf of the Dead

The living are constantly digging us up for forensic purposes,
to discover where things went wrong, for them, not us.
They haul us out of the grave when we are chatting

with neighbours, eavesdropping on visitors above, or in a deep
sleep. This can happen when they are on the loo
or have just finished sex; most often we are dragged

in front of the family and told how badly we let them down
or how poorly we brought them up.
When they are done, we make our way back to lie

in our graves and wait in turn for the grave-digger
to shovel the soil back on us, and ask him
to pack it hard, really hard, like cement.

The Gorbals Palace

It was a signal when the Comanches appeared
and the wagon train formed an O
in the Saturday matinee
for the Braves in the Stalls to attack the Cowboys
up in the Circle. Half-chewed toffees were fired
as fast as a hand-gun could unload.
Rubber bands launched gobstoppers.
Ice-cream cones were filled with piss.

It was worse than Custer's Last Stand.
Braves went to The Happy Hunting Ground.
Cowboys fell. The film would halt
when Many Horses leapt onto the stage
and did a War Dance.
The National Anthem stirred blood.
Those in the Circle stood for 'God Save the Queen',
whilst we in the Stalls sang the Irish national anthem,
threw Cokes back like firewater.

The Marching Season

That God might assist Uncle Hugh in abstaining
from drink forced mother, father and me to do
decades of the rosary. We were on our knees
when a band outside brought us to our feet.

From the cradle we had been warned to steer
clear of these people, not to pray for them,
in case they outnumbered us when we ascended
into Heaven. They were Protestants playing

The Sash My Father Wore. Uncle Hugh,
opposite, had hung the Irish flag
out of his tenement window. The band halted,
the music continued. Men in orange sashes

dashed into Hugh's close and set the flag alight.
To commemorate this act, kerbs and sills
were painted green, white and gold,
flags on poles were bolted to chimneys.

The Pope and Saint Marx

Back then, every Catholic home possessed a picture of Pope John
XXIII. Some had lights that flashed, it was said,
to the rhythm of his heart. Most men in these households
were thankful for the light this cast which aided them
during the night to empty their bladders.

Mother's brother, Hugh, had two pictures, side by side:
one was the Pope, the other Saint Marx as Hugh called him.
Both were leaders of millions, he said. One was to assist us
into Heaven, the other to enable us to take what we were due
on Earth. This, the priest informed me at confession

was a mischievous notion. We prayed God would give me
extra guidance as I encountered such people as Hugh.

The Pay Poke

Only the shadows of the two men crossed the doorway.
I peeled father's pay poke open, laid out his wages in piles.
The first man was from a loan company.
No words were exchanged. He was with someone
who looked like 'The Hulk'. We included him
in our prayers. The second man was a priest.
God was his minder. Purses and wallets opened
for him like the sea for Moses. He was paid
in silver. We felt special when he gave the house
a blessing, called each of us by our name.

So it continued until mother became the man
of the house; father's heart had had enough.
I would spill out her wages, wait for the rap.
I often wished I had a beanstalk. Now I set aside
money: for the men from 'The Chemist' in the block
who provide us with snort, the hard cases back
from Iraq, who provide security on the estate,
and those who come with the Labour Party's plate.

Parable

When the priest stood in the pulpit,
the congregation's prayers gathered speed
like the engines on a Houston rocket.

We prayed that he be thrust to Heaven,
cast down for siding with the shipyard owners.

He denounced as Communists
those who aided the striking workers.

God moves hands in many ways.
The collection plate was empty for weeks.

Part of the flock moved to graze
on an ungodly plain.

The priest, with a Bishop and a live-in
housekeeper to keep,
spoke no more on these Earthly matters.

The Lead Thieves

While the congregation prayed
my father and brother stripped
lead from the church roof,

rolled it into tiny prayer mats,
then inched back down to spend Sunday
boiling lead. They would cast

religious figurines,
display them on their web site:
Arsenius the Weeping Monk,

Agnes invoked for chastity,
Eloi the saint of metal workers,
Jude for hopeless causes.

When they scale God's roofs
in bad weather may the patron saint
of thieves protect them.

The Aisle to Heaven

As all the other boys slept, I scaled dykes and walls
to lift the great rusted ring on the church door
God left open and don the black robe, the white surplice
so stiff it could stand unaided. I would light the beeswax
candles and wonder how many bees it took to make one
as I waited for the priest to appear and nod for me

to proceed to the altar. I'd place the plate
beneath the chins of neighbours to catch the wafers
that might fall. The priest would go off to breakfast.
Mother stood at the christening font with pails.
We'd race each other, swinging our mops,
washing the aisle to Heaven.

The Dark Stuff

It's in a crossroads village like this
Kavanagh said poetry is made,
and just as I was about to fade

into the darkness of Biddy Jack's
for a pint of black and open a fresh
pack of cards with the boys in the back,

a tractor spilled its load of turf
like a spray of surf onto the road,
revealing a gun horde and,

this being where it was, three onlookers made
the sign of the cross, loaded the trailer
and, with a nod, the old fella drove off, forcing me

to sit at the bar, absorb the shock
and ponder whether poetry is made or not.

The Promised One
2 May 1997

We encountered Tories on a no-go estate
at the corner of Whig Street and Prig Street.
We were both canvassing for our candidates.
You could cut the hatred with the edge of a leaflet.

If it hadn't been for a top-knot bobby on a bicycle
we would have truncheoned the Tories
with more than our tongues.

It's a conflict as old as the Bible:
two tribes warring over tablets of wisdom
to control hands and words.

Whilst the electorate slept after having drawn
an X we the disciples paced
like an expecting parent, convinced
we were about to deliver 'The Promised One'.

Fathers' Day

I swore at the hospital staff,
demanded relief from peritonitis,
whilst father, without a sound,

went down. At home,
behind the bathroom door,
by force or prayer

mother was unable to shift
his weight. What passed between
them, I do not know.

Out of that darkness
I was tumbling into I can still feel
his grip.

A transfusion took place.
My hand grew warm,
his turned cold.

The Handshake Test

I steer away from love
that has a firm handshake.

Give me a hand
which will topple a body

with the lightest touch.

Meeting under Mussolini

It was the custom in medieval Italy
to hang crooks by one foot.

Mussolini hung by two boots from a meat hook
outside this café in Milan.

Neither of us plans to play the role
of an avenging partisan.

We steer from revealing infidelities
which might force us to hand

over our wedding bands
and be left to hang

alongside the ghost of Mussolini,
and his henchman.

We sip on what led us here,
to renew our vows in the Vatican.

The Visitation

Before sunset she led me into the water,
the way lovers wade knowingly,
declared the sea a font for blessing flesh.

A voice from Heaven called her name.

There were flashing lights, a sound
like police cars, ambulances,
helicopters, unacceptable language.

Darling

I know you'd like to tattoo your name
on my body.

We all need proof we're not
insignificant.

I prefer something that washes off
when you go.

If We Should Part

Let me leave first. I won't expect sympathy
but hope you'll accede, now and then,
to physical intimacy.

Let me pack your night-shirt from Lahore
a comforter to keep mental health workers
from putting in the door;

let me take photos, videos on my phone,
to upload and play on the flat screen
when I'm alone.

I would appreciate your silk brassiere-
a hammock for the kittens,
Arthur and Guinevere.

Evidence for a Divorce

I want to put on a white hooded suit, overshoes and gloves,
to gather evidence, scan your phone and laptop,
dust your body for fingerprints. Instead,

I've bought a clear plastic bag, handcuffs and ankle cuffs,
a see-through cling film costume to lure you
into the shower, bag your head, cuff your wrists

and ankles. I want to cart you onto the building site opposite
with your Pomegranate & Fig Essence,
run you that long-deserved bath of concrete.

Nursery am

The divorce rate is soaring in the home corner.
Land-mines and dead soldiers fill the sand-pit.

A tangerine is rolled into the toilet and a child
makes a noise like a grenade. A tongue is used

like a baton to cosh a nursery bully. At break-
time we discover the milk in the water-tray,

dolls being bathed. At home time a child
is asleep, a boy leans over her to kiss her,

like a scene from a fairy-tale. The children's
shrieks bring the Headmaster running.

In the foyer, mums come and go with children
clutching paintings that resemble Guernica.

The Day They Announced the Earth was Going to Die

Had anyone else heard the news?
I squirmed all day in the classroom
as if about to hear the spelling test results,
waited for mother to whisk me home.

Dad would be back early. We'd have to be brave
like the man in the wireless had said.
There would be no Ark. It would be sudden.

I had chewed the end off my pencil as I waited
for Mrs. Boyle to dismiss us, award everyone
a gold star. At home time, mother asked,
'What's the matter?' I didn't answer.

Dad hadn't arrived. I unplugged the radio,
made mum tea and sat on her lap.
I was very brave. There was six minutes to go.

The Earth Has Lost its Bloom

We are not here to stand and debate
the climate, the economy.
The earth will not wait.

We are not here to stand and judge
your eel-like tongue,
we have listened to you fudge.

We are not here to wave
as you flee on your ark into space.
We are here to take back what the Earth gave:

the hives and bees, the flowers and seeds,
how things are displayed
on our children's frieze.

Piloting Pennies

Our pockets are full of two-penny pieces
when we go to a demo. I sand the edges

until they're as thin as a popadom.
They are ideal for skimming

above the heads of police, splitting
the foreheads of BNP -ers.

In the right hands, like Ahmed's,
they can reach a speed of sixty miles per hour.

If you want to have a go,
we practice in the park, on flowers.

Ahmed was a star. He could take the head
off a sunflower, extinguish a fag

in a mouth from twenty yards.
He should have been a bowler for Pakistan;

instead, he's bringing 'brothers' down
in Afghanistan.

At the Unemployed Recruitment Centre

We sat in a row as if we'd been sent to the Deputy Head
to be belted by his tongue and told we would
end up in Afghanistan, or on the dole, be holding
babies before we drove on a road.

Most of us failed the army recruitment test.
Now we were only fit for burglary or daytime TV;
having our name scratched on the tower block

alongside people who had overdosed. Father's words
finally make sense: 'A reserve labour force
is essential to push wages down. We are
the economy's toilet roll'.

Ageism: an Exemplary Worker

Ageism aids the economy,
it plucks old 'whiteheads'
from the labour force,
discards 'wrinklies'
from the front face of services
and replaces them with
a shapely body.

'Oldies' are dispatched
to park benches,
voluntary work in hospitals,
and 'Care Homes'
where medication turns
their world off,
leaves them on trolleys,
or tortures them
in day centre rooms.

Agesim never ages,
it supports widespread
euthanasia and is happy
to deal with those who clog
the arteries of the living.
It looks forward to winter
when pavements are icy,
homes become cooler than morgues;
and would never flop
into a rocking chair or
consider a pension plan.

It recalls when life expectancy
was poor, vaccines unavailable,
and wishes only to assist
those who have stopped feeling
good in their skin,
dread anniversaries,
wetting themselves.
Ageism is always on the lookout
for those who walk past
the house where they live.

Newsworthy

I have seen allotment keepers bunch
like bees in a hive to prevent grass
being covered in tarmac;

workers race like paramedics to where
a capitalist axe was raised;

seen a pinstripe hunched over a laptop
being saved by a kid in a hoodie
from a switch-blade,

and what could have been his mate
give up a seat for an old lady.

Capitalism Has to be Applauded

Capitalism is a grafter that never takes breaks
or arrives late; requires no passport
and has no eye for colour, race.
Its wallet has a thirst for profit.
It rarely asks for an early morning call
and measures success in the rise of stocks and shares.

We should celebrate how it fills our fridges,
our minds: applauds our contribution
to making it strong by being a good employee
and voting for the Party which will serve it well.

Capitalism awards Governments a second term
in office for introducing bills to make us work longer
for less, freezing our pay to enable it to regain
strength when it is poorly.
It never applies for sick leave or a vacation,
just needs a constant drip-feed
of good housekeepers and cheap labour.

Wars are essential in reviving it.
The production of arms forces the unemployed
into work and into an army uniform.
It resuscitates churches, develops sites
for graveyards, gives us a Remembrance Day.

We should devise an anthem in its honour:
swear an oath of allegiance,
wake to a national alarm call,
have an annual celebration.

Capitalism is an inspiration,
it grants peerages and offices.
Each day at work should be an audition.

The Happiness Factory

I want to be an employee in The Factory of Happiness,
where I will work all shifts, never complain
about the going rate, foremen raising daily quotas,
security guards frisking us at the gate.

I want to earn an employee-of-the-month badge,
have strangers shake my hand seeing
The Factory of Happiness stamped on overalls
I will wear daily after work.

I want the evening news broadcaster to announce:
'Today, The Factory of Happiness surpassed
all targets. Surgeries and hospitals are empty.
Production plants will open all over the country.'

The Land Rush

This planet has more owners of title-deeds than trees.
There is no land to claim, no tribes to move,
herds to rustle. The stock-markets are private poker clubs.
We need the pioneering spirit, set out on horseback

across the sky with canteens of whiskey, rifles,
clouds for bedrolls. We need to file claims on new planets.
Who will ride with me? I am payrolled by Virgin

and BT. I have posts, barbed wire, horses that would have
outrun Seabiscuit. There will be no sheriffs,
only us and the vast prairie of darkness.
We will drill and build, ride home high in the saddle,

to a fanfare of trumpets, saddle-bags stuffed
with stars, singing 'Home on the Range'.

Aladdin's: Purveyors of People, Products, Pastures

Welcome to Aladdin's, with more wonders on sale
than a genie could create. Let us take your mind off
on our flying carpet. Our first lot is this Olympian athlete.
His organs are ready to be plucked out, frozen
or transplanted. It is a body in the bank, I say.
Who will bring my hammer down?
Go home with their future body parts?

What am I bid for this solar-driven factory?
It comes in a flat-pack, complete with workers
as dependable as robots but more versatile.
They are programmable and require little maintenance.
They will reproduce your future work-force
and are tagged to be dispatched to any site
on the planet. I have a reserve price.
Who will start an avalanche of bidding?

Lot three is this hospital on the screen,
inclusive of patients. It has waiting-lists
that will keep investors happy and a twenty-four-
hour conveyor belt system that is fully robotic
at surgery level. The profits will clear your arteries.
The staff have a microchip in their brain
to keep them up-to-date with the patients'
medical history. Who will aid my recovery
from the previous offers?

The last lot of the day is Africa,
where business has been slow to graze.
Where your colleagues can play Hunt
The Locals and keep their catch to show back home.
The continent comes with its own security force,
remote-controlled, fitted with web cams.
Its inhabitants will be sold at a later date.
Who will leave with the deeds of the world's
largest estate? Who will close the door on today?

Tic

Whilst he covets the attention of the TV interviewer,
and being considered as a Government front-bench runner,
his mother, Lady Paris Smith

notices a facial tic not inherited from his father
but of a prominent Cabinet Minister
she once cross-partied with.

Left, Right Left…

Maybe the creation of Left and Right
was caused by a full-on argument with God
in Eden or by a stone wall built round a field,

two brothers in the Old Testament,
or the emergence of a Spartacus type.

This we know: there is need on one side,
greed on the other; our stomachs expand
or shrink to what they know.

Anthems, arms and flags accumulate
in history's wardrobe.

Art in Ascendancy

On the eve of the Government's party conference,
we gathered outside the hall not to hold a vigil

but as artists to spray our dismay. Walls are our catwalks,
our mouthpiece. We donned Davy lamps, finished

before the sky's light came on, proud our hands
had found a tongue for those without a voice.

The media pronounced it a renaissance in art.
The Minister for Arts proffered a 'Yes, but…'

We have an unofficial project list that includes the turrets
of Tower Bridge, Tate Modern's chimneys and walls…

The Parliamentary Blacksmiths

Wouldn't it be wonderful if during their term in office
Ministers used their tongues like wands
to legislate that houses, schools and playgrounds be built;

banks redistribute wealth; debating clubs be formed
in every workplace; and we use remote controls
on TV sets to vote on Government proposals!

Instead, they sweat like blacksmiths at the anvil
attempt to hammer us into shape.

The Minister of Poetry

A people without poetry are butterflies without wings.

Under the State of Emergency
the first act of the new Government
will be to declare a Department of Poetry
to address the growing decline
of the nation's minds.

Each day will commence with presenters
of radio and TV reciting uncomfortable
and provocative poems.
Newsflashes will bring us work
from dissenting poets.
Tabloids and broadsheets
will paste them on front pages
and schools will become centres
of poetic excellence.

Verse-makers will be employed
in every workplace to encourage
creativity and cycle
to the remotest parts to deliver
a first-class service.

Prison inmates will be paroled
when they can write and recite
verses of new intentions.

Debates in the Workers' Parliament
will be conducted in sonnets.
Airlines will attach odes
to the back of headrests.
Life-jackets will contain
inflatable haikus. Hospital
patients will be comforted
by light verse. Poetic drop-in
centres will be sited in supermarkets.

The State of Emergency will be lifted
when Presidents and Prime Ministers
from abroad stop seeking our assistance.
Anyone who enters our country
must be a published poet.

Driving to Utopia

I imagine a table laid for two on a beach, and you
being waited on by Plato and Thomas More,
insisting they desist from serving the first course.

They dim the sun, withdraw to the dunes,
while you sip a Robert Owen cocktail and text,
'Hurry, before the tide turns.'

My thumb moves into fourth gear. I ditch
the sat nav and drive, until I see 'Utopia'.
There to greet me are 'Red Shelley' and Mayakovsky.

They urge me up the driveway. The children's
screams in the rear cause me to brake
in front of Butlin's gates.

The Unacknowledged Archivist

Some collect fridge-magnets, postcards, shot-glasses.
For dad it's leaflets: not the type shoved through letterboxes,

but those handed to the masses at demonstrations,
picket lines, occupations, the unofficial history

of why people take to the street, a record of protests
and demands he trims and pastes, labels and dates in albums

and then leaves on the coffee-table.
Leaflets that won't be packed in crates and hauled

to a collectors' fair. He has made us swear they will not
be a job-lot on e-bay or dropped in the recycling bin

but stored in the eaves until the National Museum
of Labour forwards a request to put them on display

or in the unlikely event an interest is expressed via us,
his children: Karl, Rosa, and me, Zapata Villa…

The Planetary Commission

What is it like now on Earth, Commander?

The earthlings walk upright, use tongues to stab and slash.
They have drawn imaginary lines across the planet
and declared, This is mine!

And what is their future, Commander?

A new class will emerge. Planet Earth will be declared
a Heritage Site. Barbed wire, tanks and guns
will be exhibited in museums.

Did you find love on Earth, Commander?

The gravitational pull for love is fleeting.
Everything is conditional.
I was forced to swear vows, wear metal on a finger.

Rule, Britannia!

Yes. I can sing *Rule, Britannia!*,
stand shoulder to shoulder with Millwall supporters.
I am darker than our darkest kit
and can match racist tongues and fists.

Yes. I can sing *Rule, Britannia!*
I bleed when knifed at work by graffiti,
cry when my son is whipped
by words in the playground.

Yes. I can sing *Rule, Britannia!*,
stoke your bank account,
donate my blood and organs,
carry the flag into battle for you.

Yes. I can fight for Britannia,
watch poppies sprout from my chest.

Democracy was a Fine Idea

until the Government dragged it onto the floor
of the House of Commons, ripped
its thoughts out and held them high,
taunting the opposition.

They plucked the vision from its sockets,
tore the speech from its mouth,
severed its head
and stamped on its calloused hands.

To ensure its remains would not be venerated,
they doused it with hate, struck a match
and shovelled the ashes
down a sluice into the Thames.